P is for Pelican

A Louisiana Alphabet

Written by Anita C. Prieto and Illustrated by Laura Knorr

Sleeping Bear Press™

315 E. Eisenhower Parkway, Ste. 200
Ann Arbor, MI 48108
www.sleepingbearpress.com

Sleeping Bear Press is an imprint of Gale, a part of Cengage Learning.

10 9 8 7 6 5

Library of Congress Cataloging-in-Publication Data

Prieto, Anita C., 1933-
P is for pelican : a Louisiana alphabet / by Anita C. Prieto;
illustrated by Laura Knorr.
p. cm.
Summary: An alphabet book that introduces Louisiana's history,
culture, and landscape, from the official reptile, alligator, to zydeco.

ISBN 978-1-58536-137-3

1. Louisiana—Juvenile literature. 2. English
language—Alphabet—Juvenile literature. [1. Louisiana. 2. Alphabet.]
I. Knorr, Laura, 1971- ill. II. Title.
F369.3 .P75 2003
976.3—dc21   2003010460

Printed by China Translation & Printing Services Limited, Guangdong
Province, China. 5th printing.   10/2010

*For Scott, Tony, Jean, David, Taylor, Adam, Amanda, Casey, and Logan…
who can recite the alphabet. And for Abigail, who is just learning it.*

ANITA

*My deepest gratitude and thanks for their patience and support to Jennifer,
Barb, Heather, and the wonderful staff of Sleeping Bear Press. You're the best!*

LAURA

The alligator is the official reptile of the state of Louisiana. The word "alligator" comes from the Spanish *el lagarto*, meaning "the lizard." In the wild, alligators play an important part in wetland communities by helping to control overpopulation by wild animals.

Louisiana's alligators were almost extinct by early 1960. They were hunted for their skins, which were made into boots, shoes, wallets, purses, luggage, and belts. Then they were made an endangered species and given full protection from hunters. By 1987, the alligator population was stable.

A is for Alligator

The Alligator crawls
on a swampy trail.
He has sharp, pointy teeth
and a long, long tail.

Aa

Bb

Beignets (pronounced ben-yea) are square doughnuts without a hole in the middle. They are sold in French Market coffee shops in New Orleans, Louisiana's largest city. Acadian French settlers made these delicious pastries as long ago as the time of the Civil War.

Beignets are served warm with lots of powdered sugar sprinkled on top. It's fun to watch them being made right before your eyes. Grownups like to dunk them in *café au lait* (coffee and milk), but children like them best with a glass of cold milk. Be careful when you eat them, though, or you will end up with powdered sugar all over your face!

As you enjoy your beignets sitting in an outdoor cafe, you will see the St. Louis Cathedral in the distance. People ride by in colorful horse-drawn carriages. The Mississippi River is nearby. You might hear the music of a calliope on a pad-dle-wheel excursion boat.

B is for Beignet

Sugarcoated doughnuts
served piping hot and sweet.
Children love to eat Beignets.
What a yummy treat!

C is for Crawfish

If you walk in muddy waters
where the Crawfish grow,
be very, very careful
or they'll pinch you on the toe!

Crawfish look like tiny lobsters. But while lobsters live in the sea, crawfish live in freshwater ditches or ponds. Crawfish are three to four inches long. They have four pairs of jointed legs, which help them walk along the bottom of their shallow-water homes. When frightened, they swim backward. Have you heard the expression, "Don't crawfish out of that?" It means don't back out of something you have agreed to do.

Crawfish also have two powerful claws (pincers)—their chief weapons of defense. They can move their eyes in any direction. Two long feelers explore surrounding waters.

The crawfish is the official state crustacean. Some people in Louisiana call crawfish "crawdads." Outside of Louisiana, crawfish is usually spelled "crayfish."

C C

D is for Delta

Delta land is fertile ground,
the farmers think it's tops.
It's a perfect place for growing
a variety of crops.

Dd

Much of Louisiana was once part of an ancient inlet of the Gulf of Mexico. As the Mississippi River flowed through the area, it carried large amounts of silt (small bits of earth) into the inlet. Over thousands of years, the land was built up. Even today, as the Mississippi continues to deposit sediment, new land is being formed in south Louisiana.

The delta is the new land being formed at the mouth of a river—land that usually takes the shape of the Greek symbol "delta." This is what is happening south of New Orleans where the Mississippi forks into several directions as it empties into the Gulf of Mexico.

Sometimes this new land is called a "bird's foot delta" because it looks like the triangular shape of a bird's foot.

The overflow of the Mississippi River has made Louisiana's soil very fertile. Cotton, Louisiana yams, rice, tomatoes, strawberries, soybeans, corn, and sugarcane are some of the crops grown there.

E is for Egret

Snowy white Egrets,
what a beautiful sight,
as they rise from the water
and soar off in flight.

The snowy egret is a long-necked migrant bird with beautiful white plumage. It is one of many varieties of birds that visit the rich marshes of south Louisiana. But in the early years of the twentieth century, egrets were killed for their feathers. Soon very few birds returned to feed each year.

That's when Mr. Edward Avery McIlhenny decided to turn Avery Island into a sanctuary for egrets and all manner of birds (pelicans, spoonbills, herons, blue-winged teal, mallard, shiny black ibis). Mr. McIlhenny stocked ponds with food and brought in wagonloads of twigs and branches, which the birds used to build nests. He called his project "Bird City." Gradually, more and more birds returned to the safety of the sanctuary.

A *fais do-do* is a country dance. Young and old meet to enjoy delicious Cajun food, sing songs, and dance to lively music played by a fiddler. In French, *fais do-do* means "go to sleep." Cajun mothers put their babies to sleep with a French lullaby. Then they join their friends at the dance.

The Acadians (or Cajuns) were a group of French people who left their homeland in the 1600s and settled in Canada. They called their new home Acadia. Later, that name was changed to Nova Scotia. When the British took over in Acadia, the Cajuns were driven from their homes.

They settled in many places in America. A large group came to southwestern Louisiana where, even today, they honor their French language and customs.

F is for *Fais do-do*

At a *Fais do-do*
you'll tap your feet
and dance to the tune
of a fiddler's beat.

G is for Gulf of Mexico

What looks like a foot
with a long, funny toe
that dips into
the Gulf of Mexico?

Louisiana is a Gulf Coast state. The Gulf of Mexico plays an important role in Louisiana life. People come from all over to fish in the gulf waters, catching blue marlin, amberjack, tarpon, red snapper, king mackerel, wahoo, and many other fish. Commercial fishermen harvest oysters and trawl for shrimp offshore.

The Gulf of Mexico is a very important oil- and gas-producing region. Large offshore drilling rigs and oil production platforms are found in the gulf. These platforms also serve as artificial reef systems for marine life.

The Gulf of Mexico offers many career opportunities, too, such as Underwater Archaeologist, Marine Biologist, Oceanographer, Petroleum Engineer, and Environmental Scientist.

H is for Hurricane

Hurricane winds
are wild and strong,
they blow through the day
and all night long.

H h

Hurricanes are great whirling storms that roar across the ocean and sometimes onto land, causing great damage to property and danger to life. In different parts of the world, hurricanes are called typhoons or cyclones. A storm becomes a hurricane when its winds reach over 74 miles per hour.

Hurricanes strengthen in the tropical waters of the Gulf of Mexico, feeding on warm air. As winds increase they spiral around a central area called the "eye." The eye of a hurricane is very calm.

In 1960, the first weather satellite went into orbit, allowing meteorologists to track storms. Today, at the National Hurricane Center in Miami, Florida, computer programs create models of possible storm paths. By predicting the hurricane's path, scientists can warn people who might be in great danger.

I is for Isleños

When Isleños crossed the ocean,
they didn't know their fate.
Those courageous Spanish people
who settled in our state.

The community of Isleños (ees-lane-yos), found mainly in St. Bernard Parish, reminds us that Spain once ruled Louisiana. In 1778, to protect its interest in the New World, Spain sent over many settlers, who came from the Canary Islands. In Spanish, *isleños* means "islanders."

Even when Spain no longer held the Louisiana territory, the Isleños stayed. As their newly adopted country grew, they became farmers, expert ranchers, commercial fishermen, trappers, and hunters. They fought against the British in the War of 1812 and in other wars to protect America.

After World War II, many Isleños moved to large cities. But even today in St. Bernard Parish, the Isleño cultural identity is cherished and preserved.

I i

J is for Jackson

Hooray for General Jackson!
He fought to victory
at the Battle of New Orleans
to keep our country free.

The War of 1812 against Great Britain is sometimes called the Second War of American Independence. It lasted three years. Toward the end of the war, the British army, led by Major General Edward Pakenham, wanted to take over the city of New Orleans.

On January 8, 1815, Major General Andrew Jackson led a poorly equipped army to victory against 8,000 trained British troops. Jackson even had help from Jean Lafitte and his band of pirates, who lived in the Barataria swampland.

Andrew Jackson became a national hero. He was later elected the seventh president of the United States. Each year, on the anniversary date, Americans from all over come to the Chalmette Battlefield, a National Monument in Chalmette, Louisiana, to reenact this important battle.

Jj

K k

K is for King Cake

Who'll become a King
right before your eyes?
At a King Cake Party
it's always a surprise!

Every year, on January sixth, Louisiana children celebrate Kings' Day. In the Christian faith, this day marks the arrival of the Magi, the three Kings, at the stable in Bethlehem.

Many King Cake Parties are held. The King Cake is oval in shape and covered with delicious purple, green, and gold icing. The cake is cut with great ceremony—and much excitement—for inside is baked a small plastic "baby." Each person chooses a piece of cake, hoping to find the piece with the baby hidden inside. That lucky person becomes King or Queen of the party.

Parties continue until Mardi Gras Day. After that, the season of Lent begins, and King Cake parties are over until the following year.

Many people call the Louisiana Purchase the best real estate deal ever made. On April 30, 1803, President Thomas Jefferson agreed to pay the French Emperor, Napoleon Bonaparte, fifteen million dollars for the Louisiana Territory. That may sound like a lot of money, but it amounted to about only four cents an acre!

When it acquired this land—900,000 square miles—the United States almost doubled its size. Thirteen states were carved from the Louisiana Purchase: Louisiana, Arkansas, Colorado, Iowa, Kansas, Minnesota, Missouri, Montana, Nebraska, North and South Dakota, Oklahoma, and Wyoming.

Louisiana claims 51,843 square miles of the Louisiana Purchase. It became America's 18th state when it joined the Union on April 30, 1812. Baton Rouge is Louisiana's capital city.

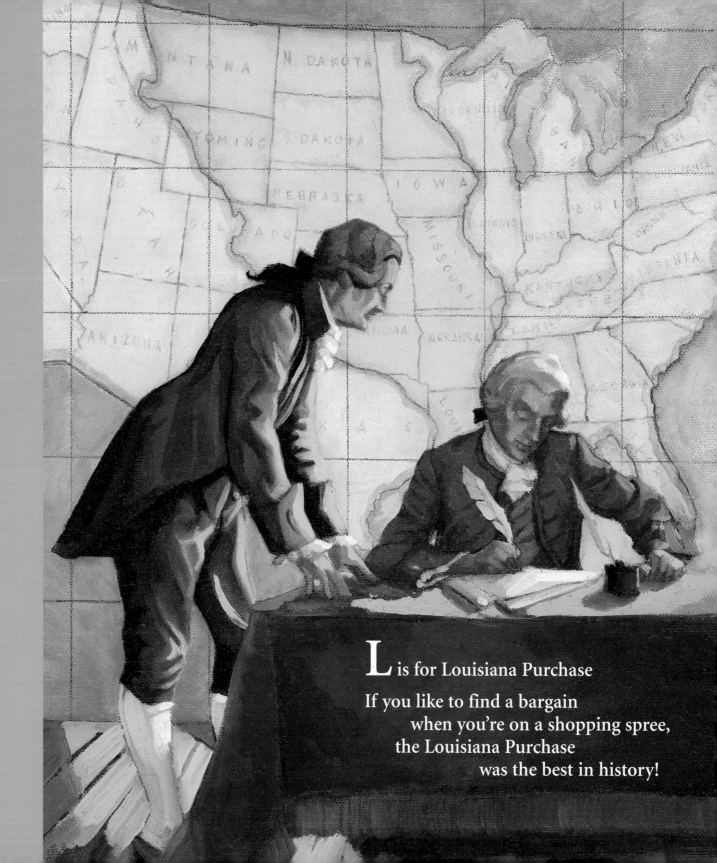

L is for Louisiana Purchase

If you like to find a bargain
     when you're on a shopping spree,
the Louisiana Purchase
          was the best in history!

People come from all over the world to celebrate Mardi Gras in New Orleans. Mardi Gras is French for "fat Tuesday." It is held on Shrove Tuesday, the day before Ash Wednesday. It is a time for having fun, because the solemn season of Lent begins the next day.

The official colors of Mardi Gras—purple (for justice), green (faith), and gold (power)—were adopted by Rex, King of Carnival, in 1892. Mardi Gras begins on Twelfth Night, January 6th. There are formal balls, parties, and parades in the days leading up to the big celebration on Mardi Gras Day. Mardi Gras is observed in many other cities and towns in Louisiana.

m
M

M is for Mardi Gras

Parades and lovely costumes,
bands that lead the way,
that's what always happens
on Mardi Gras Day!

N is for Nutria

There's a really ugly critter
that has made its nest
in Louisiana marshlands.
The Nutria's quite a pest!

The nutria is a rodent. It has brown fur, small ears, webbed hind feet, a long skinny tail, and big orange buck-teeth. Some nutria weigh as much as 20 pounds. They live along riverbanks, in lakes, marshes, and ponds. When they invade an area, they crowd out native animals, damage crops, and accelerate erosion.

The nutria was introduced into Louisiana from Argentina to be raised for its fur. Unfortunately, some of the animals escaped into the surrounding marshlands. In five years, the rodent spread across the southern part of the state. Nutria have moved to many parts of the United States. The prob-lem is so great that a Congressional committee is looking into ways to control this destructive creature.

O is for Oyster

Suppose you open an Oyster,
and right before your eyes,
you see a lovely, shiny pearl—
Oh, what a nice surprise!

Oysters are invertebrates, meaning they have no backbone. They belong to the mollusk family just like clams, scallops, and mussels. An oyster has two hard shells held together by a strong muscle. It opens its shell just a little bit to feed on tiny plants and animals floating in the water.

Oysters are grown in "beds" in coastal waters. Louisiana is ranked as one of the country's top oyster producers. More than 250 million pounds of in-shell oysters are harvested every year, approximately 50% of the nation's total oyster production.

Pearls are the only gemstone produced from a living organism. Sometimes a foreign object (like a grain of sand) slips inside the oyster's shell, which irritates the oyster. To protect itself, the oyster coats the object with layers of nacre (mother-of-pearl). After a time, a beautiful pearl is formed.

Oo

P is for Pelican

The Pelican is a funny bird—
It catches its food in a pouch,
and when it's stuffed with a heavy load,
I'll bet that poor bird says "Ouch!"

Pp

The eastern brown pelican is Louisiana's state bird. Both the state seal and the state flag show a mother pelican feeding her babies.

Two kinds of pelicans live in Louisiana—the American white pelican and the eastern brown, which nests there in much greater numbers. The pelican has been part of Louisiana's history since 1704, when a French ship named *The Pelican* arrived on Louisiana shores. It is thought that William C.C. Claiborne, first governor of Louisiana, decided to put a pelican on the state seal.

The pelican has a large bill and an expandable pouch, and a wingspan of six feet or more. Pelicans fly over shallow waters on the southern United States coastline or in sheltered inlets. Nests are usually found on the ground, on rocky stretches of islands, and even in low trees.

Louisiana has dozens of festivals each year and dozens of festival queens. Festivals celebrate many things: local crops, people, customs, etc...They may last a weekend or even longer. People come from all over to eat spicy Louisiana foods, dance to lively music, see local crafts, play games, and enjoy the fun.

Some examples of festivals are the Ponchatoula Strawberry Festival, the Walker Bluegrass Spring Festival, and the Etouffee Festival held in Arnaudville, Louisiana. Others are the Ruston Peach Festival, the Des Allemands Catfish Festival, the Ville Platte Cotton Festival, the Louisiana Yambilee held in Opelousas, and the Holiday in Dixie celebrated in Shreveport and Bossier City.

Q is for Queen

Pretend you're a Queen
with a sparkling crown
whirling about
in your beautiful gown.

There are many old plantations in Louisiana. Rosedown is one of the most beautiful. Its major crop was cotton. Located in St. Francisville, Rosedown was built in 1835 by Daniel and Martha Turnbull. The house has tall columns and sweeping galleries (porches) typical of most antebellum homes. Mr. Turnbull spared no expense in bringing to Rosedown the finest things available. Furnishings were imported from the North and also from Europe. A 28-acre formal garden still blooms today.

Rosedown, a window to plantation life in the 1800s, contains 85% of its original furnishings. It has been named a Louisiana Historic Site.

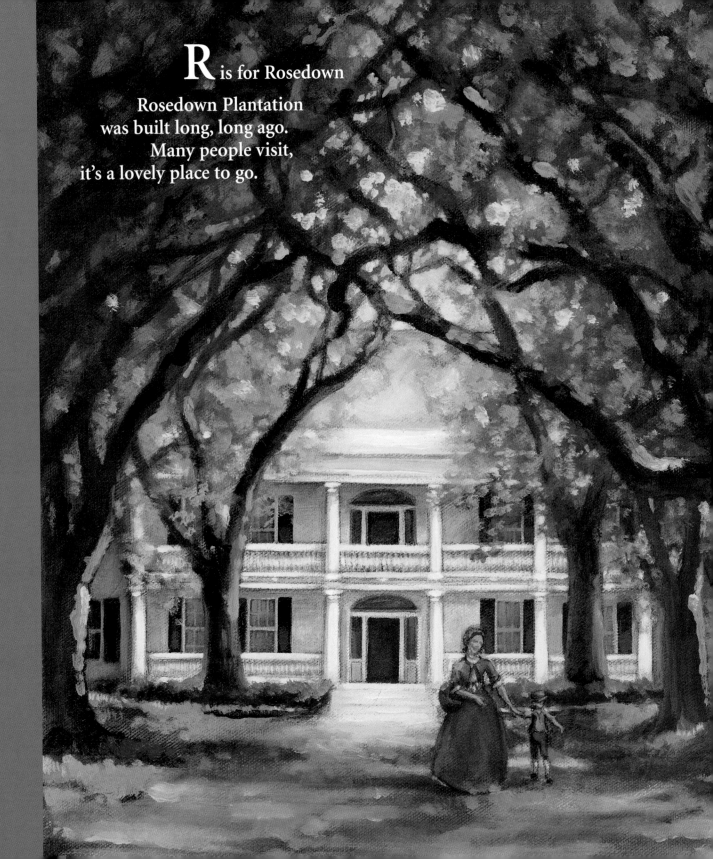

R is for Rosedown

Rosedown Plantation
was built long, long ago.
Many people visit,
it's a lovely place to go.

S is for Superdome

The Superdome's a sight to see,
it's big and tall and round.
It looks like a giant mushroom
in the middle of the town.

The Louisiana Superdome opened August 3, 1975. The "Dome" is used on many different occasions. This covered arena is perfect for football games and other major sporting events. The Super Bowl has been held there many times.

The Dome is also great for conventions, concerts, and large meetings. When a carnival ball is held there, huge floats roll in off the streets, circle the Dome floor, and have lots of room to spare. Even the circus plays there when it comes to town.

When Pope John Paul II visited New Orleans in 1987, 80,000 schoolchildren, their parents, and teachers came to see him at the Superdome.

Ss

T is for Tarpon Rodeo

This rodeo is different:
No bucking broncos here,
but if you catch the biggest fish
everyone will cheer.

Tt

Every July fishermen come from all over to take part in the annual Grand Isle International Tarpon Rodeo, an exciting fishing competition, which lasts three days. Each day, fishermen sail out to see who can catch the largest fish.

The tarpon is a large silvery game fish found in warm coastal waters. In addition to tarpon, other fish (sailfish, barracuda, amberjack, red snapper, and many others) are caught at the rodeo. On the last day, prizes are given for the largest catch in each category.

Grand Isle, Louisiana, is a barrier island—an elongated piece of land that runs parallel to the mainland. It serves as a buffer, protecting the mainland from strong offshore winds and rough, damaging surf. It also serves as a refuge for wildlife. The Grand Isle community numbers about 1,500 people. During the Tarpon Rodeo there are more than 12,000 tourists.

Louisiana's climate is hot, humid, and subtropical. It is one of the wettest states in the country. The average yearly rainfall is 57 inches. That's a lot of rain!

Much of the New Orleans area sits, like a big saucer, five to eight feet below sea level. When it rains, water cannot drain away normally. There are many pumping systems, with workers on duty all day and all night. The systems pump rainwater through underground canals—some large enough to drive a bus through. The water is pumped into Lake Pontchartrain. It takes a lot of work to keep Metropolitan New Orleans from flooding.

U u

U is for Umbrella

Don't forget your Umbrella
    when the weather gets hot.
On Louisiana summer days
it really rains a lot!

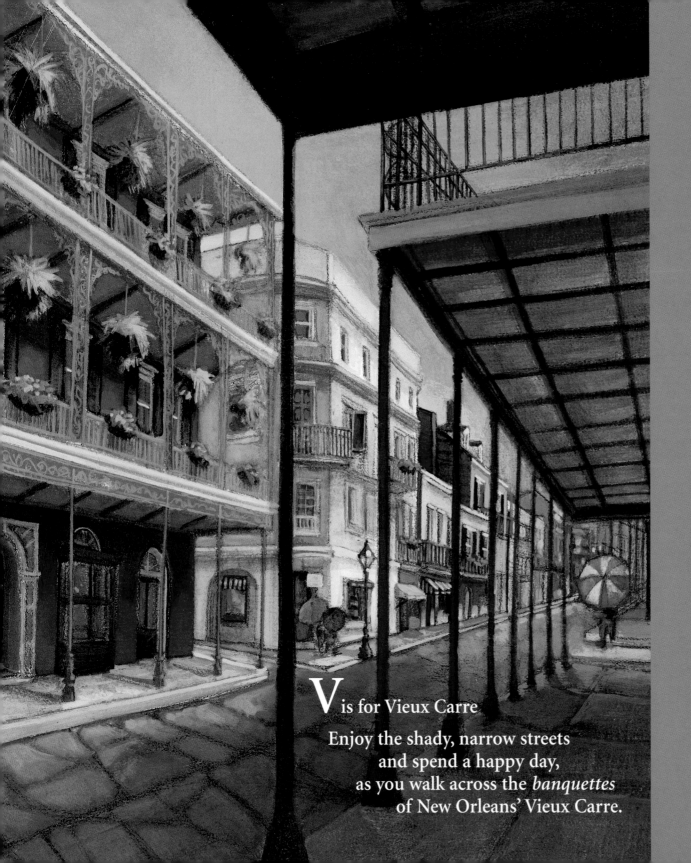

V

V is for Vieux Carre

Enjoy the shady, narrow streets
and spend a happy day,
as you walk across the *banquettes*
of New Orleans' Vieux Carre.

The Vieux Carre (Old Square) is also called the French Quarter. This six-by-twelve-block area is the original city of New Orleans, settled by the French. The narrow streets are lined with small Creole cottages, art galleries, and gift shops. Many homes and stores have lovely wrought iron balconies decorated with hanging baskets of bright red geraniums, ferns, or begonias.

Even the street names in the Vieux Carre tell stories. Iberville Street, Bienville, Toulouse, Ursuline, Governor Nichols, Burgundy, St. Peter, and St. Ann Streets all remind the visitor of the area's French history. Some people still call the sidewalks "banquettes," a name from the French language.

Jackson Square, the St. Louis Cathedral, and the Cabildo (seat of government under Spanish rule) are all found in the Vieux Carre.

Louisiana depends on its waterways. The mighty Mississippi River, called the Father of Waters, flows 569 miles through Louisiana as it makes its way to the Gulf of Mexico.

The Sabine River is part of the Texas-Louisiana boundary. The Pearl River forms part of the boundary with the state of Mississippi. Other important rivers are the Red, Calcasieu, Atchafalaya, and the Ouachita.

In Louisiana, slow-moving streams are called bayous. Other waterways are Lake Pontchartrain, the Mississippi River Gulf Outlet (a 76-mile canal to the Gulf), and the Intracoastal Waterway. The Bonnet Carre spillway is a kind of waterway opened when the Mississippi River gets too high. The spillway allows water to flow from the river into Lake Pontchartrain, saving the area from flooding.

W is for Waterways

Water, water everywhere,
it flows throughout our state.
It's part of everything we do,
it helps to make us great.

Mother Katharine Drexel, a Catholic nun who established the Sisters of the Blessed Sacrament, opened Xavier University of Louisiana in 1925. Mother Katharine used her own money to begin many schools for Native American and African-American students. In the year 2000, Pope John Paul II officially canonized her in a ceremony in St. Peter's Square in Rome, Italy, and she became Saint Katharine Drexel.

Xavier University is open to qualified students of every race and religion. Accredited by the Southern Association of Colleges and Schools, it is known for its excellent College of Pharmacy. In 1995 the university was chosen to participate in the National Science Foundation's Model Institutions for Excellence in Science, Engineering, and Mathematics program.

X is for Xavier University

At Xavier University
you'll like everyone you meet,
and you'll get an education
that is very hard to beat.

Y is for Yams

Colorful to look at,
delicious and sweet,
Louisiana Yams
are so good to eat.

When the first French settlers came to Louisiana, they found Native Americans—the Alabama, Choctaw, and Opelousas tribes—growing sweet potatoes, which soon became a favorite food of the settlers, too.

Sweet potatoes are an important Louisiana crop. Grown on many farms of southwest Louisiana, they can also be found growing throughout the state. Often called "Louisiana yams," sweet potatoes belong to the tuber family. They grow underground. Their deep, golden color indicates a high beta-carotene content. Sweet potatoes are rich in vitamins A and C, potassium, and fiber.

The yam crop is harvested in late summer and fall. Each year in October, the city of Opelousas holds a Yambilee Festival to celebrate the harvesting of its Louisiana yam crop.

Zydeco is the traditional music of Black Creoles of southwest Louisiana. It is a mixture of Afro-Caribbean rhythm, old-time blues, and Cajun music. An accordion leads a zydeco band. Other instruments are drums, guitar, rubbord, bass, and sometimes a fiddle. A rubbord is a curious instrument made of metal. It hangs from the shoulders and is scraped with a metal spoon to provide a rasping background beat.

The Zulu Social Aid and Pleasure Club is one of the leading African-American social groups in Louisiana. The organization gives Christmas baskets to needy families and donates money and time to many community organizations. On Mardi Gras Day, Zulu parades just before the Rex Carnival organization, and its floats are among the most beautiful seen through the entire carnival season.

Zz

Z is for Zydeco

This book is almost over
and I know that you'll agree,
when you read about Zulu and Zydeco,
you'll have gone from A to Z.

Pelican Puzzlers

1. What does the word "alligator" mean in Spanish?

2. In what city would you find the St. Louis Cathedral and the French Market?

3. What is the nickname of the state of Louisiana?

4. Where is Bird City?

5. What large body of water is south of Louisiana?

6. When does a tropical storm become a hurricane?

7. Who led American troops against the British army at the Chalmette Battlefield during the War of 1812?

8. What do you call the center of a hurricane, where the winds are still?

9. What country sold Louisiana to the United States in the Louisiana Purchase of 1803?

10. What is the Vieux Carre?

11. Why is Bonnet Carre spillway important?

12. What is a rubbord?

13. Parts of 13 states were created from the Louisiana Purchase. Can you name at least five of these states?

14. What is a *fais do-do*?

1. "Alligator" comes from the Spanish *el lagarto* meaning "the lizard."

2. New Orleans

3. The Pelican State

4. Bird City is on Avery Island in south Louisiana. It is a sanctuary for the snowy egret and many other birds.

5. The Gulf of Mexico

6. A tropical storm becomes a hurricane when its winds reach over 74 miles per hour.

7. Major General Andrew Jackson, who later became the seventh president of the United States.

8. The center of a hurricane is called the "eye."

9. Emperor Napoleon Bonaparte of France sold Louisiana to the United States.

10. The Vieux Carre means "old square." It is the name of the original city of New Orleans settled by the French.

11. The Bonnet Carre spillway is a waterway that is opened when the Mississippi River gets too high. When the spillway is opened, water flows into Lake Pontchartrain, saving the area from flooding.

12. A rubboard is a curious musical instrument used in a zydeco band. It is made of metal, hangs from the shoulders, and is scraped with a spoon to make its musical sound.

13. The 13 states were Arkansas, Colorado, Iowa, Kansas, Louisiana, Minnesota, Missouri, Montana, Nebraska, North and South Dakota, Oklahoma, and Wyoming.

14. A *fais do-do* is a country dance. In French, *fais do-do* means "go to sleep."

Anita C. Prieto

Anita C. Prieto was born in New Orleans, Louisiana, and now lives in Metairie. From Louisiana State University she has a B.S. in Education and an M.Ed. in Educational Administration. Her doctorate (Ed.D.) is from the University of New Orleans. Her professional life (33 years) was spent in the Orleans Parish School System where she worked as a classroom teacher, television teacher, school principal, and acting area superintendent. She is now retired and writing full-time. Her favorite pastimes include traveling, reading, gardening, and playing Mah-Jongg with friends.

Laura Knorr

Artist Laura Knorr graduated with a Bachelor of Fine Arts degree in Illustration from the Ringling School of Art and Design in Sarasota, Florida, and has worked as a freelance illustrator for several years. Laura lives in Commerce, Georgia. *P is for Pelican* is her second children's book with Sleeping Bear Press. She also illustrated *K is for Keystone: A Pennsylvania Alphabet*.